CW01650979

Sports value course

Coaching young people to play sport and own clear values

Tim Perry with Susannah Pilkington

Dedicated to:

Meggie, Joy and Hattie – what a gift you are!

David and Judith Pilkington – thank you for your unending love and faithfulness in prayer. You have trained me in the way I should go.

First published 2003
ISBN 1 85999 6485

Scripture Union, 207–209 Queensway, Bletchley, Milton Keynes, MK2 2EB, England.
Email: info@scriptureunion.org.uk
Website: www.scriptureunion.org.uk

Scripture Union Australia,
Locked Bag 2, Central Coast Business Centre, NSW 2252
Website: www.su.org.au

Scripture Union USA
PO Box 987, Valley Forge, PA 19482
www.scriptureunion.org

British Library Cataloguing-in-Publication data.
A catalogue record of this book is available from the British Library.

Printed and bound in Malta by Interprint Ltd.

Cover design: Martin Lore

Contents

Introduction

Welcome to the Sports Value Course!

A large proportion of people get great enjoyment from sport in some way, whether that's from spectating, taking part recreationally or playing competitively. This makes sport an amazing means of engaging with people, both young and old. It can provide a point of reference that people are comfortable with and understand. Using sport in your group's sessions can add an extra dimension.

The *Sports Value Course* has been designed for youth leaders whose groups enjoy sport. It is a ten-week course that provides hour-long sessions which aim to teach life values alongside the coaching and playing of a sport each week. There's a brief biblical basis for each value, and ideas about how to begin to look at each value with the group and facilitate discussion. Then there are tried and tested activity ideas that will help every youth leader feel confident about the fun sports coaching they include in each session.

Young people face tremendous challenges in the world in which they live. In order for them to grow and develop – not simply survive, but mature and thrive – clear values for sport and life are crucial. Though Jesus Christ was not well known for his sporting ability, there's no greater example of one whose life reflects such clear values. The values addressed in the *Sports Value Course* are based on his life and teaching.

Rev Tim Perry and Susannah Pilkington

Elements of the course

Teaching the values/issues

The role of the coach

One of the best ways you, as a coach, are going to teach the values covered in the course is by living them out. If you feel daunted by that, don't, because God's promise to us all, through Jesus, is that by his Holy Spirit he will be seen in our lives (Galatians 5). So allow the Holy Spirit to fill you afresh (John 14). Aim to be humble in the way you conduct yourself, treating those present with dignity; be fair to one and all, and be a leader in the way you live out your life.

A Introduction to each value

It is important that you read the introduction to each value covered before you take the session. The intention of this introduction is to help you think through the issue being addressed and to give you a biblical basis for the topic. It should provoke thought before the session rather than be for you to use directly as you teach; Part B is for that.

B Session plans

Each value covered in the *Sports Value Course* is based on the life and teaching of Jesus. Many people use the course with young people from outside the church. We want those present to see the difference that Jesus can make to life, but we don't want to force the point. So, when you begin to bring Jesus into the discussion, using Part B, do it in a natural, non-threatening way. As well as giving an idea of how to discuss the value, Part B provides a suggested coaching session plan that seeks to link the 'physical focus' and the value being covered.

Format

The general format for each session is:

- Warm up/skill
- Introduction/stretch
- Skill (if not part of the warm up)
- Game 1
- Sports focus
- Game 2
- Life focus
- Game 3
- Conclusion/wrap up/cool down and stretch

This format is intended to be flexible, and there will be times when various elements can be combined. However, certain elements should be consistent throughout the sessions and should be retained even if the rest of the physical programme is adapted.

Warm up/cool down

We all know that warming up and cooling down are important for all physical activity. However, when time gets tight they can be the first things to be missed out. Rather than letting this happen, use the warm up activity to reinforce what has been covered in a previous lesson or even teach a new skill for the current session. Also use this time to promote teamwork, build relationships and affirm individuals.

Warm up activities should be gentle, should gradually raise the pulse rate and body temperature and be done before any stretching. Warm up activities which also introduce the skills being taught are provided for each session.

Cool down activities help to gradually bring the pulse rate back down towards normal resting levels. They also help the circulation carry any by-products of the exercise such as lactic acid away from the muscles and therefore decrease later stiffness. The easiest cool down simply involves going for a gentle jog, then bringing it down to a walk before stopping to stretch.

Stretching

Research has suggested that stretching after the activity, as part of the cool down, is more important that stretching before the activity; don't forget to stretch at the end as well as the beginning!

It is vital to **remember the ethos** that we are trying to promote throughout the sessions. Use the warm up and skills time to build teamwork, encouraging the young people to use each other's names and work with a variety of people. Also, the way that the leader treats the group will serve as an example for the young people. This means it is crucial to take time to affirm and encourage everyone, particularly when someone is not doing very well.

Teaching a skill

Each session involves some work on developing a sports skill. The skill taught obviously needs to be adjusted to the different levels of your group. Suggestions are provided as to how to introduce and develop the skills. This is a great opportunity to build teamwork.

Games/activities

The important aspect of game play in the *Sports Value Course* is not only that you play the sport, but also that you apply to the game what you have been talking about in the session. In the session on 'Winning with humility', for example, you want to help the young people to learn how to win well, with humility. It is not simply that you want those present at the end to be able to applaud those who have lost, recognising their part in the game, nor to realise that boasting about winning is unhelpful to the loser, though both of these are important. It is about unpacking what it means to win well – things like giving encouragement, playing fairly within the rules and communicating effectively. These are the things you should see coming through your session, and there will be times during game play when you will want to stop the game and pick on the areas that you feel are going well, eg great passing/communication, as well as things not going so well, eg a lack of encouragement.

Though each game in each session will be focusing on different values, these are some of the most common values to concentrate on during every session:

- **Team play** – getting each member of the team involved, reminding those in the team to pass the ball to every member, not just those who are particularly good.
- **Encouragement** – encouraging each person to support those in their team, whether they are seen to be doing well or not so well.
- **Communication** – talking to one another, using each other's names.
- **Fair play** – playing within the rules.
- **Discipline** – playing fairly/working at certain skills/watching use of bad language.

Most of the sessions make use of adapted games with smaller numbers of players in the teams for game play. The idea is that games with small teams allow each young person to be involved in the game. Can you remember eleven-a-side football/hockey where you hardly ever got to touch the ball? However, the desire to keep the teams small has to be weighed against the desire not to have young people sitting off for too long. Each leader will need to make a decision about team size, taking numbers and space available into account. If you do need to have larger teams, and it is resulting in some young people being left out, introduce some criteria that mean all the team gets involved (eg every team member must have touched the ball before their team can shoot). Clearly each leader should feel free to adapt the use of small teams to suit their group and the facilities they have at their disposal.

Sports/Life focus

In each session, Sports focus looks at how the value covered relates to the sports arena, while Life focus relates it to life in general. (There will be overlap, but generally speaking attempt to help the young people focus on each area separately.)

Practical suggestions for leading Sports focus and Life focus
Ask those present to sit on the floor. You want them to be comfortable for the next few minutes, to listen and interact.

Learn the names of each person in the group as quickly as possible and use them! This will affirm each person, and also enable you to keep control if necessary.

Try as much as possible to get everyone in the group to contribute. There will be some who want to speak, whilst others will hold back. Be sensitive to both, enabling those who want to contribute to be able to do so, but also allowing those who feel less secure to share when the time is right. It may be in the second, third or fourth session where this happens. By using names, you can direct questions to particular individuals. If you sense someone is shy, get to know them before you direct a question to them.

Be clear in your own mind where the session is going before you ask the questions. Use the session plan initially as a guide; in time you will become confident enough to adapt the session as and how you want, but at the beginning, use it because it has been tried and tested.

Always attempt to affirm people by thanking them for their answers and encouraging them. When you need to bring order, try to do it in a way that does not undermine one particular individual. If necessary, talk to that individual later, but don't cause them to stand out in the group. Praise in public, reprimand in private!

Try to incorporate humour. We want those present to enjoy coming to the session.

Spotlight on the Bible
This section is a snapshot of what the Bible has to say about the value being covered. Use this if you are working with churched young people, or if it is appropriate to increase the amount of 'God' content in the session.

Other things to think about

• Safety should be a top priority. One area of safety that is often overlooked is where the equipment not being used is kept during the session. For example, put spare balls into a bag rather than having them rolling all over the playing area. This also helps to reduce the amount of equipment lost.

• Take time to consider how you are going to start and finish the session. If the young people arrive in dribs and drabs you may need to have an activity that they can do that will simply occupy them until you are ready to start. However, remember that this activity will set the tone for the session; if you let them simply mess about it will be harder to get them to do what you tell them to when you start. At the end, it is wise to ask the young people to help collect in and put away any equipment neatly. This can save considerable clearing up time!

• Please note that all timings are only guidelines. Generally, the sessions will be very full; it is better to plan too much than too little but know what you want to cut if time is tight – you don't want to miss out the point of the session!

• Guided discovery is a teaching approach that involves using questions and answers to lead the group to the points you are trying to make. It is very useful as it helps to keep the group 'tuned in' to what you're saying. It also helps to motivate them as they will be more ready to work on areas that need improvement if they have identified them for themselves.

• Positive reinforcement of the behaviour and sporting skills you are focusing on is vital. Make sure you tell people specifically what you are praising them for: 'That's good team work', 'Great pass', 'Well done for looking up', 'Good back up in defence' etc.

• Reality checks should feature in each session and can be placed at any point. They are a time for the young people to be honest with themselves and realistic about how much they apply the value in everyday life. This will probably be an area that each leader will want to to tailor to their particular group. Suggested questions are provided.

Session 1

Winning with humility

A Winning is seen as an attractive thing to aspire to, whether in sport or in life. Everyone enjoys winning. Getting the best exam results or a promotion, being the head of school, coming first in a race – winning is a good thing as it gives us a sense of satisfaction for a job well done. Winning is an important ingredient for an individual to build their confidence, but how we win is just as important, and that is the focus for this session.

You can win, yet not value yourself for the way you have won, perhaps because you've cheated or pushed people out of the way in your bid for success. You can win, and forget that your gifts come ultimately from God, and receive the adulation with no thought of him. You can win, and have no concern for the person who has lost, who has worked just as hard as you, yet hasn't received the prize of victory.

Humility is an important ingredient when it comes to winning and winning well. For many, though, humility is seen as weakness – letting someone go first, or recognising how small we are before God, doesn't seem conducive to getting to the top. But humility speaks of strength – to appreciate other people's gifts means to be secure in our own; to say sorry speaks of being able to look honestly at ourselves; not boasting about our successes speaks of an inner recognition of our worth and of other people's worth too.

The Bible places a high regard on humility, saying:

> *'Do nothing out of selfish ambition or vain conceit, but in humility consider others better than yourselves. Each of you should look not only to your own interests, but also to the interests of others. Your attitude should be the same as that of Christ Jesus.' (Philippians 2:3–5)*

Quite a challenge!

Jesus Christ was a great example when it came to humility (Philippians 2:6–8), from the way he lived – treating those around him as equally important and special – to being prepared to die a criminal's death for a crime he never committed. Yet Jesus wasn't weak, he was strong; he didn't lack ambition, he was ambitious for all that was good.

Humility reminds us that our gifts and the ability to play sport comes from God. Humility reminds us that although we may enjoy the privilege of winning, there are others who experience the pain of losing. Humility enables us to enjoy the success of winning with our feet firmly on the ground.

Sport – Football

Football, the beautiful game! Former Liverpool manager Bill Shankley is famously quoted as saying, 'Some people think football is a matter of life and death ... I can assure them it is much more serious than that.'

Football is by far the most widely played and watched team sport in this country, and there are very few people who are immune to the football culture in the UK – just look at the response during the World Cup. However, the football players who reach iconic status are not necessarily always the role models we might choose for our young people. Trouble off the pitch is widely reported, and often their on-the-pitch behaviour is far from what we might aim for as we think about 'Christian sporting attitudes'. The problem is that, due to the high profile of football, what young people see footballers doing will play a key role in what they think sportsmanship is all about. This means that it is especially difficult for young people to come up with a sporting attitude that is different to the one they see displayed by the professionals, and it is VITAL that we seek to apply the values we address to football.

B Value

Winning with humility

Physical focus

Football, dribbling, ball control

Game play priorities

Encouragement, fair play, teamwork

Aim

To recognise the value of humility.

Learning objectives

To recognise that:

- winning is a good thing
- the way you win is just as important as winning itself
- humility plays a crucial role in this.

Equipment required

Footballs (preferably enough for one each); goals or cones to mark goals; bibs; cones to mark playing areas and use in warm up; a whistle.

Warm up and skill

Close ball control (5 mins)

If you don't have enough footballs for one each, you will need to gear the warm up and races in Game 1 accordingly, eg divide the group into the number of teams that you have footballs for.

Give each person a ball and ask them to keep it close to them within a marked area without bumping into each other. The area should have enough space for them to move about relatively quickly, but be small enough so they have to keep the ball close and keep weaving in and out of each other. As soon as they seem to have got the hang of this, let them know that you are going to run in and out and kick their ball out of the area if they let it get too far away from them. Add in other elements, eg they have to turn 180° when you blow a whistle once, swap balls with someone else when you blow it twice etc.

If you don't have enough footballs, use a whistle blow to signify swapping the ball with someone who doesn't have one. Those without footballs can also try to kick loose balls out of the area – not tackling the other players, just kicking the ball away if it is not close enough to them.

Stretch (4 mins)
Mobilise all joints and stretch all muscles that will be used during the session. Hold each stretch for 6–10 seconds.

Introduction

Introduce yourself, and say how the *Sports Value Course* works, talking about today's value, winning with humility, using the material given (see Part A). Define the word humility, offering practical examples: not boasting about success, saying sorry, congratulating someone for doing better in something than ourselves etc.

Game 1

Dribbling/passing races (8 mins)
Use this time to promote teamwork, build relationships and affirm individuals.

Ideas:

• Dribble the ball around your partner, return to where you started, pass them the ball, they dribble around you. Ten passes and sit down.

• In fours, with two on each side, run, keeping the ball under close control, to the first person in the opposite queue and join the back of that line. Eight times across (which should get them back to starting positions) and sit down.

• Set up cones to have relay races, dribbling in and out, with them passing back to the next person when they get to a certain spot.

• Stand in a circle and pass the ball around it. See how many times you can pass it around the circle in the time it takes for someone to run around the outside, keeping a ball under close control. (This will hopefully also demonstrate that it is quicker to pass than to run with the ball.)

As winning with humility is the value this session, make sure you point out who wins each race.

Try to emphasise the following teaching points as appropriate. Practise using both feet to dribble. It's important to look up – both when dribbling or when going to pass – as in a game you will need to be able to check to see where your teammates are and where the defenders are. Use the inside of your foot for passing. Control the ball before you try to pass it.

Sports focus

Winning and sport (8 mins)
Bring everyone together and sit down. Ask those present if they enjoy winning at sport/board games etc. What do they enjoy about winning? Receive answers with affirmation.

Key point – winning is a good thing! It's OK to enjoy winning!

Remind those present why winning is a good thing, tying in with what they themselves have said. It **gives a good feeling, builds confidence, tells us how good we are at something** and **is a reward for hard work**.

Go on to say that just as winning is a good thing, so is the way we win. We need to win well, both in the way we play and in the attitude we have. Ask the question 'What is a good way to win in sport?' and give an example, eg trying our hardest. At the end, add (if not already given): **playing fairly – playing to the rules**; **enjoying ourselves – not taking it too seriously**; **having humility**.

Focus on what it means to win with humility. Ask how we can win with humility. How can we win well? Add if not already given: **recognising our opponent and their part in the game – sportsmanship**; **recognising our gift of sport comes from God**; **recognising that there are times when we will lose**; **not boasting when winning and making someone else feel small for losing**; **congratulating others who win or lose**; **treating others as equals**.

Explain that in this sports session you want to see some of these qualities of 'winning well' coming out.

Game 2

3 v 1 passing game (8 mins)
Get into groups of four, and mark out each group's playing area. Three attackers have to make five passes in a row to score a 'goal'. The defender is not allowed to tackle the person with the ball, but tries to either intercept a pass or force the attackers to make a bad pass that goes out of the area. If this happens, the defender gets a goal. The first to three goals wins. The attackers can dribble the ball if this is going to get them into a better position to pass. Once a team has won, a different person becomes the defender and they play again. Having the defender wear a bib makes it easier.

Adjust the number of passes required for a goal as appropriate, depending on the skill of the group. The more skillful the group, the more passes they will be able to manage. However, many groups may find getting even three passes very difficult.

As winning with humility is the value this session, make sure you note who wins/loses each game – the defender or the attackers. Also, don't forget to reinforce the game play priorities when you see them during the game.

Life focus

Winning and life! (8 mins)
Bring everyone together and sit down. Ask how we might win in life, if necessary giving examples, eg **being made captain of a team, being head of school, coming top of the class for an exam, being a good friend**.

Ask the group how they can win well in life, eg **working hard at school, being fair and honest in what they do, being humble**.

Unpack how they can win humbly in life, eg **by receiving success graciously, treating others as equally important, using our success for the good of others, recognising and respecting other people's achievements, recognising God as the giver of life, thanking him for our successes**.

Game 3

Football (10 mins)
Play a game of football, encouraging them to use the skills they've been working on – close ball control and passing. The numbers you have in each team will be dependent on how much room/equipment you have. If possible, you should have everybody playing. Don't have too many on a team, otherwise some will not get to touch the ball much. Don't make the playing area too small, otherwise there will be no space for teams to be able to spread out and pass the ball to each other.

Again, don't forget the game play priorities, encouragement, fair play and teamwork. Positively reinforce these when you see them during the game.

Cool down and wrap up

Don't forget to stretch!

Spotlight on the Bible

Winning is good and we should enjoy it. However, we shouldn't think that winning makes us better than others, or try to win in order to put others down. The Bible says,

'Do nothing out of selfish ambition or vain conceit, but in humility consider others better than yourselves. Each of you should look not only to your own interests, but also to the interests of others. Your attitude should be the same as that of Christ Jesus.' (Philippians 2:3–5)

Reality check

'Do I need to change the way I act when I win?'

'Do I manage to win well in my everyday life, at home, at school, with my friends?'

'What did I do well this week?'

'What can I improve on for next week?'

Session 2

Losing with dignity

A Losing is something we will all experience at some point in our life. Whether we are the greatest sportsperson or the most intelligent person ever to set foot on the planet, we will experience losing. We won't always get the position of our choice in the school team, or the promotion we want at work. Losing happens to us all. Today's session deals with the fact that it's OK to lose, but also addresses how we lose, and how we can lose with dignity.

To have dignity means 'to recognise one's true worth'. The Bible reminds us how valuable we are:

> *'For God so loved the world that he gave his one and only Son that whoever believes in him shall not perish but have eternal life.' (John 3:16)*

This session looks at losing well, and at the fact that our value as an individual does not depend on winning. How many times have you seen someone stomp off the court or refuse to shake an opponent's hand? Perhaps one of the reasons why they find it hard to lose is because they haven't learnt about their own true value, or that of other people – success has been the basis of that value. Today the all-prevailing attitude seems to be 'if you win, you feel good about yourself; if you lose, you feel bad about yourself'. However, if you struggle to value yourself, you will struggle to value others too. So how can we lose with dignity?

Firstly, we need to learn to value ourselves before we even step onto the tennis court or rugby pitch. This is the amazing difference that Jesus makes, reminding each of us that we are important, special and unique, made in the image of God who loves us and cares for us as his own children (Romans 8:15). It is not because of anything we have done or will achieve, but because he chooses to. When Jesus is baptised, before he has done anything of significance in his ministry, God tells him how much he loves him (Matthew 3:17). Jesus knew his value before he had accomplished anything.

Secondly, we should play to the best of our ability. If we do that and still lose, we can value ourselves for having done all that we could possibly do, even though it wasn't good enough to win. Often the temptation when we are losing is to cheat, but winning through cheating only ends up with us devaluing ourselves all the more. All too often, if cheating plays a part in getting us to the top, whether it be in sport (through things like taking drugs) or life (like acting dishonestly), our world can come tumbling down on top of us.

Thirdly, we can lose with dignity by congratulating those who have won. Our time for winning will come, but in the meantime we need to be able to say 'well done' when someone else wins.

Sport – Unihoc

Originating in Sweden, Unihoc takes elements of field and ice hockey to make a safe yet physically demanding game that can be played indoors by both men and women. It uses plastic sticks with flat heads and either a plastic puck or a light ball. The sticks, like those used in ice hockey, can be used on either side making it very easy for young people to play. It is now played in twenty countries worldwide and most secondary schools and sports centres have equipment that could be borrowed or hired.

Depending on the space you are playing in, you can chose if you want to play off the walls (like five-a-side football) or have the pitch boundaries of normal hockey. Unihoc is fast and furious and, for safety's sake, it may be worth reminding group members that they aren't playing golf and therefore don't have to swing their sticks wildly!

B

Value

Losing with dignity

Physical focus

Passing

Game play priorities

Not giving up, applauding the winner, fair play and encouragement

Aim

To help group members to see their true value.

Learning objectives

To recognise:

- that everyone loses in sport and life.
- that losing doesn't mean failure.
- our true worth as individuals and other people's worth.

Equipment required

Unihoc sticks and balls/pucks (one each – know how to adapt any practices if balls are in short supply though. Depending on the ability of the group, slower balls are easier to control. They should not be too light, otherwise it is too easy for them to be lifted off the floor); goals or cones to mark goals; bibs; cones to mark playing areas and use in warm up; a whistle.

Warm up

For the first unihoc session, let the young people play and practise their unihoc skills while you wait for everybody to arrive. This gives you an opportunity to assess their ability.

Introduction and stretch

Mobilise all joints and stretch all muscles that will be used during the session. Hold each stretch for 6–10 seconds.

Whilst stretching, recap what you did last week. What do they remember about winning? What did they discover about football?

Using the material given in Part A, explain that today you'll be looking at a value that makes a real difference – losing with dignity.

Begin by asking whether anyone knows what the word dignity means? Accept all answers with affirmation and then give the the proper definition: 'to recognise one's true worth'.

Skill

Push pass (5 mins)

Because this is the first session of unihoc, you may want to start by telling the group what teaching points you are looking for (see below). However, you could set them off passing back and forth in pairs and ask them to try to work out what the teaching points should be in order to make a good accurate push pass. After a few minutes of experimentation, ask them what they've come up with.

Teaching points to emphasise:

- **Stance** – sideways on.

- **Grip** – in unihoc you can use both sides of the stick, however in hockey left-handed sticks are very rare, so encourage left hand at the top, right hand halfway down.

- **Look** – it's amazing how many people pass the ball without looking to see where they should be passing it to.

- **Technique** – start with the stick against the ball and push it in the direction you want it to go. This technique is perfectly adequate even to get the ball/puck to go a long way. Remind them that they aren't playing golf, and the stick never needs to come higher than knee level. This is also a safety factor.

- **Control** – control the ball before you try to pass it on.

Let them practise in pairs, going around helping, encouraging and correcting individuals as necessary.

Game 1

3 v 1 passing game (8 mins)
As Game 2 in Session 1, except playing unihoc.

As losing with dignity is the value for this session, make sure you note who wins/loses each game – the defender or the attackers.

Sports focus

Losing and sport (8 mins)
Bring everyone together and sit down. Explain that you want them to think about how we can lose in sport and yet still have a sense of our true worth. Ask those present if they enjoy losing at sport. The answer will be 'No!' Ask why that is. If not already given, add: **because it makes us feel we have failed**, **it can cause us to lose confidence**, and **we prefer to win**.

Does losing make you a better or worse person? It doesn't mean that we are failures if we lose, because everyone loses at some point, and we can develop as people through losing.

Ask how we can lose at sport and still feel good about ourselves. **By knowing we have tried our hardest**; **by playing within the rules**; **by knowing our true value before we play – God's view of us doesn't change whether we win or lose**; **by recognising the role of others in the game**; **by showing sportsmanship – being gracious in defeat and applauding the winners**; and **by encouraging others who lose**.

As they reflect on 'losing with dignity', point out and encourage this session's game play priorities:

- Not giving up – we should try our hardest.

- To applaud the winner – after a goal, at the end of a game, to encourage those who lost, to applaud those who won.

- Fair play – not only physically, but also in what is said.

- Encouragement – affirm those who make mistakes with words of encouragement.

Point out the values you are looking for in the next game session and positively reinforce them when they occur.

Game 2

Passing races (8 mins)
In the last game, despite being outnumbered three to one, the defender usually wins. This is partly to do with attacking tactics, but often due to poor passing. Go back to practising passing, but make it more fun by including a competitive element.

There are numerous passing races you can devise. Examples include:

• Ten passes back and forth between pairs and sit down.

• Pass the ball, then run around your partner, and back to where you started. They pass the ball to you and do the same. Ten passes and sit down.

• In fours, with two on each side, pass the ball to the first person in the opposite line and join the back of that queue. Eight passes across (which should get them back to starting positions) and sit down.

• Stand in a circle and pass the ball around it. Give each person in the group the chance to see if they can run around the outside of the circle faster than the ball can be passed around.

Be creative! Again, make sure there is a clear winner/loser. Are they managing to win/lose well?

NB All the above involve passing to someone who is stationary. Passing to someone who is moving is much harder, and can be included when the group is capable of it.

Life focus

Losing with dignity in life (8 mins)
Ask the group when they might feel they have lost in life. Add, if not already mentioned: **not doing as well as someone else in an exam; losing a girlfriend/boyfriend to someone else; losing a parent through death or divorce; missing out on promotion at school or work; not have getting into the college or university of their choice.**

Ask how they can lose with dignity in life and still feel good about themselves: **by trying their hardest – it can be tempting to cheat in order to win** (think of an example of somebody who has cheated); **by building others up; by recognising and applauding the success of others; by realising that failure does not make us any worse a person; by recognising that everyone loses at some point; by accepting our true worth in God; by being aware that God has a plan for our lives.**

Game 3

Unihoc (10 mins)
As Game 3 from Session 1, except now playing unihoc.

Encourage them to use what they've been working on, eg passing.

Don't forget the game play priorities – not giving up, applauding the winner, fair play and encouragement. Positively reinforce these when you see them during the game.

Cool down and wrap up

Don't forget to stretch!

Spotlight on the Bible

When Jesus died on the cross, to all who were there it would have seemed like he had lost – they didn't yet understand that he would rise from the dead, making it the biggest victory the world has ever seen! And yet the way in which he 'lost' was amazing.

And when the centurion, who stood there in front of Jesus, heard his cry and saw how he died, he said, 'Surely this man was the Son of God!' (Mark 15:39)

The way we lose will impact those around us.

Reality check

'Do I have a healthy attitude to losing?'

'What can I do to improve my attitude to losing?'

'Is there anything I need to change about the way I lose?'

'Do I manage to learn and improve from losing?'

'Do I encourage others and still value them when they lose?'

Session 3

Fair play

A Can you imagine playing a sport where there are no rules? Imagine playing rugby and being able to do whatever you like – with no rules for how you can tackle, how you can pass the ball, what is classified as in or out etc. It would be chaos! Similarly, can you imagine living in a world where you can do whatever you like? A world where you can do whatever you want to anyone who annoys you, where there are no driving restrictions and you can drive as fast as you like. We need certain rules to enable us to play sport and live life fairly.

Whether we like them or not, rules show us how to play a game, but they also give us the freedom to enjoy a game. Rules, whether they are from a parent, or from a school, are all too often seen in a negative light. Perhaps the key question for many is who sets the rules.

In sport it is relatively simple, as the rules are set by sporting governing bodies. FIFA, for example, sets the rules for football, the RFU for rugby. But who sets the rules for life?

The Bible makes it clear that God gave us rules to live by, not so that we might feel burdened by them or so that they might ruin our lives, but so that we might know how to live life as God intended. Many of today's laws for living are based on God's laws and in particular the Ten Commandments. These were given to the people of Israel after they were set free from the slavery of Egypt, and can be found in Exodus 20. Jesus came to fulfil the law, and the way Jesus lived, and the teaching he gave (especially the Sermon on the Mount in Matthew 5) should be an example to each of us of how to live today.

How can we play by the rules when it comes to sport and life? This session focuses on two areas:

1) Recognising what the rules are. Only then can we be expected to play/live by them. Jesus' life is an example for each one of us to follow; he played by the rules and he can help us to do the same.

2) Applying the rules to our lives. The temptation all too often is to break the rules – to take out someone's legs on the football pitch, to call the ball out wrongly on the tennis court, or to treat someone unfairly in life. However, the reality is that if we play unfairly, we end up hurting ourselves as much as anyone else.

Fair play enables us to enjoy and get the most out of a game/life, it enables others to enjoy sport/life, and it causes us and others to respect who we are.

Sport – Basketball

Basketball is experiencing major growth in this country with increasing free access to outdoor courts, and has a definite 'cool factor' attached to it. Dr James Naismith invented basketball in 1891. The aim was to devise a new indoor game that would provide an 'athletic distraction' for a rowdy class at the YMCA in Springfield, Massachusetts, USA, and take their minds off the New England winter.

It was originally played with nine players on each side, and the aim was to score by shooting into old peach baskets that were nailed to the lower rail of the gym balcony – hence 'basket' ball. It became an Olympic sport in 1936 and is now played by more than 300 million people worldwide.

B

Value

Fair play

Physical focus

Dribbling

Game play priorities

Fair play – in the way we play physically, in keeping the rules, and in the way we speak to other players.

Aim

To help group members play fairly.

Learning objectives

To recognise the need for rules and to understand what they are in both sport and life.

Equipment required

Baskets (think in advance how you will split the group around baskets for games); basketballs (preferably one each, but know how to adapt any practices if balls are in short supply); bibs; cones/hoops to make extra game areas if necessary; a whistle.

Warm up and skill

Dribbling (5 mins)

Follow the leader – the young people should copy what you do with the ball. Dribble with your right hand, left hand, sit down, dribble ball around feet, lie down, sit up, kneel, stand up, dribble in a figure of eight around legs etc. If your dribbling skills could do with improvement, you could ask one of the group to be the leader.

This gets the young people to stretch their ball handling skills and gives you a chance to assess their ability.

Introduction and stretch

Mobilise all joints and stretch all muscles that will be used during the session. Hold each stretch for 6–10 seconds. Whilst stretching, recap what you have done in previous weeks. What can they remember?

Also, ask why we warm up and stretch: to prepare the body for exercise, to prepare the mind for the game, to reduce the risk of injury. Not raising the heart rate and body temperature before stretching could pull a muscle.

Introduce this week's sports value – fair play – using the material given in Part A.

Game 1

Ball handling races (8 mins)
Individually or in pairs/small groups, run some races designed to improve ball control.

Examples:

- Across the sports hall and back dribbling right hand.
- Across the sports hall and back dribbling left hand.
- Across the sports hall right hand, back left hand.
- Across right hand, stop, pass ball around waist three times, back left hand.
- Across right hand, stop, pass ball in figure of eight around legs three times, back left hand.
- Across right hand, stop, throw ball over head and catch it behind your back three times, back left hand.
- Across right hand, stop, bounce ball from front to back between legs, catching it behind three times, back left hand.
- Across right hand, stop, bounce ball from back to front between legs three times, back left hand.

Don't forget the game play priorities. This session they are fair play – in the way we play physically, in keeping the rules and in the way we speak to other players. Positively reinforce these when you see them occur.

Sports focus

Fair play and sport (8 mins)
Bring everyone together and sit down. Begin with the question 'Why do we need rules when we play sport?' Add if not suggested: **rules help us to enjoy a game** (give an example of playing a game without rules); **rules tell us the way we should play a game – they act as a guide**; **rules define what is and isn't allowed, and help us distinguish between right and wrong; rules help us to play fairly**.

Ask what happens when we break rules and don't play fairly – **chaos, penalty to opposition, injury to self and others, we are not being fair to the people we are playing with**.

As they reflect on 'fair play', point out and encourage the game play priorities that you are particularly looking out for in the game.

Game 2

Basketball (8 mins)
Say that you are going to play basketball but without any of the usual rules. If your group will naturally abide by the rules, you may need to have previously prompted a couple of members of the group to break the rules by running with the ball, kicking the ball, fouling the other team etc.

After a few minutes, bring everyone together and talk about what they have experienced, explaining why rules and fair play are necessary. Go on to explain what you want to see in this game. Fair play – in the way we play physically, in keeping the rules and in the way we speak to other players.

Dribble war
Go on to play dribble war. In this, players have to dribble their ball continuously. If they lose control of it, they are out. They have lost control if they stop bouncing their ball, they go outside of the defined playing area (the playing area should be reduced as the numbers drop), they use both hands at the same time to bounce the ball or they have to catch the ball to keep it under control (both break the double dribble rule).

As well as dribbling their own ball, each player tries to make their opponents lose control of their basketballs, eg by knocking it out of the playing area. This game can be played individually or in teams, with each team working together to defend/attack. If you play in teams, the team of the last surviving player wins.

NB If you don't have enough balls for one each, half the group could play dribble war while the others play half court (as in Game 3) and swap over for Game 3.

Life focus

Fair play and life! (8 mins)
Bring everyone together and sit down. Ask the group what rules we have to follow in life, eg **how fast we drive, how we treat people, going to school**.

Where do we find these rules? **In the Bible – the Ten Commandments, Jesus' teaching and the New Testament letters; the law of the land** (the basis of which comes from the Ten Commandments); **parents/friends – we hope**!

Ask why we need rules in life: **to guide us**; **to help us distinguish between what is right and wrong; to give us the freedom to enjoy life; to help us treat others fairly**. Key point – **rules are positive, not negative**.

Game 3

Half court 3 v 3 (10 mins)
As the name suggests, this game is played with two teams of three on half a basketball court. The team in possession of the ball attack the basket. If the defenders intercept the ball or get a rebound, they must take the ball outside of the three-point line before they can start to attack.

If necessary, some games can be played by trying to get the ball to bounce in a hoop. Make sure groups rotate to all play on the proper baskets at some stage, though.

NB Basketball is non-contact! Players are not allowed to reach across or around the person with the ball.

If someone tackles unfairly, uses bad language or doesn't play by the rules, punish the team involved by giving their opponents a point. This underlines the fact that when we don't play fairly, we not only hurt ourselves but also those around us.

Cool down and wrap up

Don't forget to stretch!

Spotlight on the Bible

Obeying God is one thing, but do we have to pay attention to other rules? Sometimes it is difficult to understand why we have to keep rules set by school, parents, clubs etc. However, the Bible makes it clear that people in authority are there because God has allowed it.

> *'Everyone must submit himself to the governing authorities, for there is no authority except that which God has established. The authorities that exist have been established by God.' (Romans 13:1)*

Reality check

'Do I agree that playing by the rules is important?'

'In sport, do I play by the rules even when nobody is looking?'

'In life, do I play by the rules? At school? At home? With my friends?'

'Is there a specific area where I want to make sure I keep the rules in future?'

Session 4

Teamwork

A Being part of a team can be a positive or negative experience. However, we live in a world where, like it or not, we are called to work together. Teamwork is key for positive and effective living, whether it be within a family, at work or on a sports pitch. Young people should see teamwork as a necessary and positive value.

Teamwork lay at the heart of Jesus' ministry. He saw the value of being part of a team – we need to as well.

'Calling the Twelve to him, he sent them out two by two...' (Mark 6:7)

This session looks at what constitutes positive teamwork, pulling out three particular areas.

Firstly, **commitment**: all of us, at some point or another, think of giving up on the people around us, whether it be a person in the team who just can't catch the ball or a member of our family who continually lets us down. Things like these test our patience and make us question our commitment to that person. Commitment in teamwork is learning to work with the strengths and weaknesses of people around us, while also recognising our own weaknesses. Jesus was committed to his team – there were many times when they let him down, but Jesus continued to be committed to them just as they were to him, and also to each other.

Secondly, **encouragement**: negative criticism knocks a person down and makes them feel small, often destroying confidence and taking away self-worth. Encouragement on the other hand builds a person up. Jesus constantly reminded his disciples of how special they were, and what they were able to achieve in his name, and it's incredible to read what they accomplished.

Thirdly, a **shared end goal**: to be in an effective team, there has to be a common sense of where the team is heading. When it comes to sport, the question very often is 'Do we want to win?' but it might be 'Do we want to make sure we have all enjoyed the game?' If everybody has that same desire, then great things can happen. If only a few do, and a few don't really care, then problems occur. Jesus was clear that to be a part of his team, people need to follow him and to work with him, and one another, in achieving all he came to do (establishing God's kingdom in people's lives).

Sport – Danish longball

It is unclear whether Danish longball actually originated in Denmark. However, it is clear that the game is tried and tested, and that young people love it. Danish longball is a batting and fielding game that has been passed down between PE teachers and youth workers.

As they get the hang of the rules, young people should be encouraged to think tactically – when should they try to hit the ball long or short? When should those waiting in the safe area try to run back? How can the fielders be arranged to make it as hard as possible for the batters?

B Value

Teamwork

Physical focus

Fielding

Game play priorities

Encouragement, teamwork, communication

Aim

To help group members recognise the value of being a positive team member.

Learning objectives

To:

- recognise the difference between a positive and negative team member.
- recognise and learn how to encourage and share with others.
- apply these values to life – at school, home or in a sports team.

Equipment required

Balls appropriate for Danish longball (soft footballs or low pressure tennis balls – they shouldn't hurt when people get hit with them, but should still be able to be thrown); bat for Danish longball (if you're going to use one); cones to mark the safe area, bowler and batter positions; hoop to mark the 'drop zone' for the bat; bibs; a whistle.

Warm up and skill

Throwing races (5 mins)

Divide the group into teams (the numbers will be dependent on how many balls you have). Each team should form a big circle, and throw the ball to each person in order. The team that gets the ball back to the beginning first wins. Also add in the rule that the first person to start with the ball throws it, and then has to run around the circle back to their original place. Who gets back first? The ball or the person? (It should be the ball! This demonstrates that you can throw a ball faster than you can run, which is important in fielding games.)

Introduction and stretch

Ensure you mobilise all joints and stretch all muscles that will be used in the session. While you are doing this, recap what you have learned in previous weeks.

Introduce this week's sports value – teamwork – and say that you will be playing Danish longball. Bring out the game play priorities that you will be looking for:

Encouragement – verbally encouraging each other.

Teamwork/passing to each other – watching that individuals are not left out.

Communication – teams should talk to one another, using each other's names.

Game 1

Ball tag (8 mins)
Mark a playing area (not too big otherwise nobody is tagged). Two people start as catchers (depending on the ability of the group, you may need to start with three or even four). The catchers throw the ball to each other, but are not allowed to run with it (similar to netball). To catch people, they must touch them with the ball while holding it – they are not allowed to throw the ball at people. If someone steps out of the area while trying to escape, they are also caught. Once someone is caught, they join the catchers. The winner is the last person to get caught.

To begin with, this is hard. One tactic is for the catchers to focus on one person, and try to corner them. This requires good levels of quick passing, teamwork and communication and may take a few minutes to get the hang of.

Sports focus

Being a positive team member (8 mins)
Bring everyone together and sit down. Ask what some of the challenges of being part of a team are. What can be good or bad about being in a team? Eg, **people on the team not being as good as you; people with different goals – some wanting to win, others just wanting to have fun**.

What is needed for a team to work well? Receive answers with affirmation, adding if not already given: **playing as one of the team rather than as a group of individuals; sharing the same end goal; encouragement and support within the team; playing for each other; clear leadership**.

What makes a team not work well? **Doing your own thing; giving/getting negative criticism rather than helpful feedback; having no sense of direction; being leaderless; communicating with some and not others**.

Explain how in this session you want to see each team working positively – reminding them of some of the things that have been said.

Game 2

Danish longball
Divide into two equal teams, one batting, one fielding, and arrange the playing area – cones for the batter, bowler and score line, and a 'safe area' at the opposite end (see diagram below). If you only have one bat, the batter will need to drop it ready for the next batter to use. It is often a good idea to give them a hoop to drop the bat into, to prevent it from being thrown down, which can be dangerous. If necessary, add the rule that if the bat isn't dropped in the hoop, the batter is out – this helps them to focus on the importance of safety.

Choose the batting style most appropriate for your group. If you are using a low-pressure tennis ball, you can bat with your hand, a rounders bat, a cricket bat or even a tennis racquet. This will determine how easy it is to hit the ball and how far it is likely to go. If you are using a football-sized ball, you may still be able to bat with a rounders/cricket bat depending on how heavy it is. Alternatively, the ball can be rolled with the batter having to kick it.

The batting team lines up in a safe place where they will not be in the way.

The bowler bowls the ball to the batter, who has to run to the safe area, irrespective of whether or not they hit the ball. When they get to the safe area at the other end they can wait there as long as they like or come straight back to score.

The fielders try and get the batter out by either catching the ball, or by throwing the ball at them and hitting them below chest level with

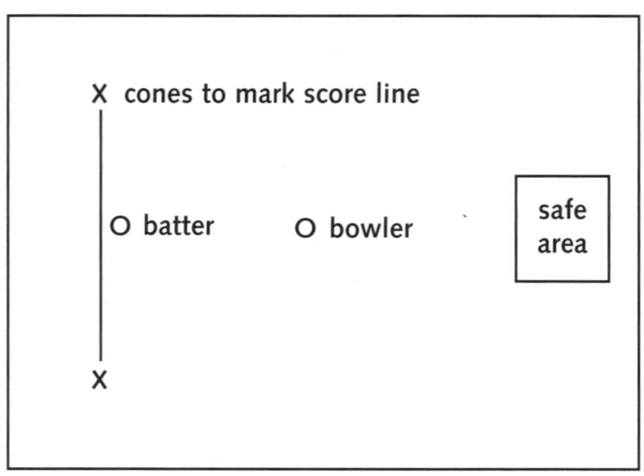

it, as they run to or from the safe area. Once a batter has left the safe area, they have to come back – they are not allowed to go in and out of the safe area – and they can then be tagged by the ball and got out.

To score, the batter has to run back passing over the score line. A team can have as many batters as they like in the safe area waiting for a good time to run back and score – however, they do need to have at least one batter back to take their turn, otherwise the whole team is out. Often five or six batters will all run back at the same time.

Decide if you are going to let each person bat a specific number of times (make sure that each person has at least one chance to bat) or whether you are going to have timed innings.

If you are playing in a sports hall, decide if you want to make a rule that batters can be caught out off the walls, or that if the ball bounces, it can be caught with one hand.

See if anyone works out that if they pass the ball to someone closer to the batter, they are far more likely to hit them. Throwing the ball at a moving target from a distance is very hard. Getting the ball to someone who is close requires a good level of quick passing, teamwork and communication, and may take a while to get the hang of.

Life focus

Team play in life (8 mins)

In what ways will we experience being a part of a team in life, eg **family, a class at school, at work**?

How might we be a negative team member in life? **By thinking only of ourselves and being selfish; by caring for certain people but not others; by not trusting those closest to us**.

How can we be a good team member? **By recognising the value of others; by encouraging and supporting others; by building others up rather than knocking them down; by recognising our need of others – God created us to need him and other people; by being a role model to others – Jesus offers that model to follow; by treating all people as equals**.

Game 3

Danish longball (10 mins)

Have a second innings of Danish longball. If the teams were very uneven use this opportunity to alter them as appropriate.

Cool down and wrap up

Don't forget to stretch!

Spotlight on the Bible

God made us and gave us particular gifts and abilities. Other people have different gifts and abilities, but everyone has a role to play if we are to achieve our maximum potential. In the Bible it describes this by likening us to different parts of the body:

> *If the whole body were an eye, where would the sense of hearing be? If the whole body were an ear, where would the sense of smell be? But in fact God has arranged the parts in the body, every one of them, just as he wanted them to be. If they were all one part, where would the body be? As it is, there are many parts, but one body. (1 Corinthians 12:17–20)*

Reality check

'Have I genuinely managed to encourage my team mates today?'

'Are there times at school or home when working as a team could make life easier?'

'Am I good at working in a team? If not, what am I going to do to try to be better at it?'

'Do I need to spend some time thinking about the 'body' – recognising that I have certain gifts and appreciating that others have different gifts?'

Session 5

Having discipline

A Discipline is a value we learn to appreciate more and more the older we get – many people do look back and wish they had worked harder at school, or had been more disciplined over what they had or hadn't said. However, discipline is not something we have to learn about later in life – it is something we can learn from an early age.

Tiger Woods is a role model for many, not simply for playing excellent golf but also for his behaviour on the course and his dedication to practise. In order for young people to excel in the sports arena today, discipline has never been needed more – the expectation of fitness and skill as well as behaviour are necessary qualities. It is not uncommon to see a sports person (young or old) cheating or going off the court sulking or swearing at the referee; these are some of the areas we want to touch on.

The Bible encourages us to be disciplined:

> *'He who ignores discipline comes to poverty and shame.' (Proverbs 13:18)*
>
> *'No discipline seems pleasant at the time, but painful. Later on, however, it produces a harvest of righteousness and peace for those who have been trained by it.' (Hebrews 12:11)*

For any child or young person to develop, whether it be in sport or in life, discipline is a necessary value, and one that we can see in the life of Jesus.

Jesus was disciplined in his day-to-day living. Why was this and what can we learn from him about living a balanced life?

Firstly, Jesus saw the necessity of spending time with God. Getting up early in the morning was important, so that he could spend time with God, talking with and listening to him. If we want something, we need to set aside time for it.

Secondly, Jesus was clear about his end goal. His purpose was to establish God's kingdom in people's lives, enabling them to know God's healing, forgiveness and peace. It is easy to focus on things in life that are not important; we need to learn to focus on what is.

Thirdly, Jesus understood the correct way to live. Although he was tempted by the devil, he stood his ground. Though others questioned him, he remained focused on what he had come to do. Though there were many times when he was tried and tested, he kept going. There will be many times in life when we will be tempted to do things that we will later regret. Learning to be disciplined, with God's help, is a key to preventing this. One of the fruits of the Holy Spirit living within us is self control (Galatians 5:23). As we invite God, by his Holy Spirit, to dwell in our lives, he will help us in the area of discipline.

Sport – Ultimate Frisbee

Frisbees originated in America in the fifties when students started throwing pie dishes to each other. Ultimate Frisbee (originally called Frisbee football) mixes the best elements of football, basketball, American football and netball, and is now played in over forty countries.

The spirit of the game is vital in Ultimate Frisbee, making it a great game to use when learning about values. Ultimate Frisbee stresses the importance of sportsmanship and fair play. Competitive play is encouraged but never at the expense of respect between players, adherence to the rules and the basic joy of play. For more information, see *www.whatisultimate.com*

B Value

Having discipline

Physical focus

General principles of attacking and defending

Game play priorities

Not giving up, fair play, working at weak areas of game, watching language

Aim

To help group members recognise the value of discipline.

Learning objectives

To:

- recognise why discipline is important.
- appreciate the positive aspect of discipline.
- apply it to life.

Equipment required

Frisbees (know how to adapt any practices if Frisbees are in short supply); bibs; cones to mark game areas and scoring zones if necessary; a whistle.

Warm up and skill

Frisbee skills/three-way weave

Give the group a chance to practise throwing and catching the Frisbees in pairs (or in a circle if you don't have enough Frisbees).

Coaching points that can help include:

- Hold and release the Frisbee so it is horizontal.
- Aim to flick your wrist as you release.
- As with all catching, it is important to move your hands in the same direction when catching to help stop the frisbee from bouncing out of your hands, and to make it more comfortable to catch.
- Catching the Frisbee by sandwiching it top and bottom can be a good way to start, particularly if the young people are scared of catching it.

Once they have got the hang of throwing and catching when stationary, get them to warm up further and try passing to someone who is moving. This can be done by using a three-way weave:

The principle behind this is rather like that of plaiting hair. Ask three people to line up and face down the pitch. The person in the middle (A) should start with the Frisbee. The person on the left (B) then runs into the middle, in front of A, and the Frisbee is thrown to them (they should preferably run on to the pass). B then throws the Frisbee to the person on the right

(C), who has run into the middle in front of them. In the meantime, A has run around the back of B out on to the left wing, before waiting and cutting back into the middle to receive the pass from C. In the same way, B then runs around the back of C on to the right wing ready to receive the pass from A. This continues all the way up the pitch.

Points you will need to emphasise about passing to people on the move are to pass in front of the person so they can run on to it. In Ultimate Frisbee, you are not allowed to run with the Frisbee. Stop and get balanced before you attempt to pass.

Introduction and stretch

Ensure you mobilise all joints and stretch all muscles that will be used in the session. You may be able to get one of the young people to lead the stretches now. At the same time, find out what they remember from previous weeks.

Introduce this week's sports value – having discipline – and say that you'll be playing Ultimate Frisbee, looking at the general principles of attacking and defending.

Game 1

Ultimate Frisbee (8 mins)

Ultimate Frisbee is an invasion game similar to football or hockey, in that each team tries to score at the other end. However, instead of goalposts, there is a scoring zone similar to American football. In order to score, a team member needs to catch the Frisbee in the scoring zone without it having hit the floor. As you are not allowed to run with the Frisbee, you have to pass it amongst your team in order to move up the pitch towards your scoring zone. Of course, the other team will be trying to intercept your passes and go in the other direction towards their zone. The team that scores the most wins.

Depending on your group, you may want to include rules such as you have to make five passes before you can shoot, or that everybody on the team must touch the Frisbee before you can shoot. This can help to ensure that all are included.

NB Don't forget the game play priorities. This session they are: **not giving up**, **fair play**, **working at weak areas of the game**, and **watching language**. Positively reinforce them when you see them occur.

Sports focus

Discipline in sport (8 mins)

Bring everyone together and sit down. Define discipline in this context. We're talking about the need to train hard, keep fit, play fairly and work on certain skills.

Ask the question 'Why do you think discipline is necessary in sport?' Receive answers with affirmation, and add if not already given: **the need to train to keep fit**; **the need to learn about the game**; **not giving away penalties**; **pacing ourselves**; **being good role models**.

How can we become disciplined? **By recognising how important it is**; **by focusing on one thing at a time**; **by setting realistic targets**; **by working at it**; **by asking God and others to help us become more disciplined**.

Game 2

Concentrate on attacking (10 mins)

Continue to play Ultimate Frisbee, but first ask the group to think about how to improve their attacking. What do they think is important when attacking? Add if not already mentioned:

- Passing the Frisbee quickly and accurately;
- Getting into space to receive the Frisbee by not crowding the Frisbee;
- Dodging defenders;

• Timing any movement and working as a team to get positioning right – not everybody should go for every pass.

Positively reinforce examples of good attacking when you see them occur. These principles for attacking apply to any invasion game.

Life focus

Discipline and life (8 mins)
Bring everyone together and sit down. Begin by asking why discipline is needed in life.

Welcome all answers and add if not already given: **it helps us to live a balanced life that combines both work and play; it helps us get things done that are important; it causes us to watch what we say and do**.

Ask 'How can we become more disciplined?' **By doing homework before going out; by keeping our room tidy; by helping out around the house; by spending money sensibly**.

Explain that God can help with discipline. He can: **help us stand up to temptation; prevent us saying things we regret later; give us wisdom to know what to be disciplined about; change us to be like Jesus**.

Game 3

Concentrate on defending (10 mins)
Continue to play Ultimate Frisbee, but ask the group to think about what they need to do as they defend and what are good ways of doing it. Encourage them to think about the different ways they defend in other invasion games (eg football, hockey, netball, rugby).

What different ways of defending can they think of? Suggest:

• Marking the person who is trying to throw;

• Marking a player to try to stop them from receiving a pass;

• Marking a space (zoning) and trying to intercept a pass.

These principles for defending apply to any invasion game.

Cool down and wrap up

Don't forget to stretch!

Spotlight on the Bible

There are many areas of Christian life that require us to have discipline: having a daily quiet time; praying for something specific; going to church when we'd rather do something else; staying out of situations that we know will bring temptations.

The Bible makes it clear that discipline is important, and likens it to the strict training that is required if you are determined to win a gold medal.

> *Therefore I do not run like a man running aimlessly; I do not fight like a man beating the air. No, I beat my body and make it my slave so that after I have preached to others, I myself will not be disqualified for the prize. (1 Corinthians 9:26,27)*

Reality check

'Do I keep going even when things get tough?'

'Can I control my language even when I lose my temper?'

'Is there an area of my life where I need to have more discipline? If yes, what can I do about it?'

Session 6

Performing under pressure

A Pressure is something we all experience at some point in our lives, whether it be in sport or in life. Young people are no different from adults, as they face increasing pressure to perform in the classroom, on the sports pitch and also have to deal with things like peer pressure.

Pressure is something we all have to live with, so the question should be how we can perform under that pressure, and in some cases, conquer it. The Bible reminds us:

'I can do everything through him who gives me strength.' (Philippians 4:13)

Jesus knew what it was to experience pressure. Even before he began his ministry, the Bible tells us he was tempted by the devil for forty days and forty nights. Throughout his ministry, he had to cope with the high expectations of those around him; and of course Jesus faced the greatest pressure of all – being crucified for a crime he did not commit. So how did he deal with that pressure?

Firstly, when Jesus was tempted, he saw it for what it was. During such times, he reminded himself of the truth found in the Bible. For all of us, there will be times when we will be under pressure from temptation. It is at such times that we need to remind ourselves to see the temptation for what it is, and bring to mind that which is true and the right action to take.

Secondly, Jesus took time out. There are many examples of Jesus taking time out of a busy day to be alone with God or to be with his friends (eg Mark 1:35, Mark 4:35). Of course, when we are in the middle of a sports match and feeling the pressure, we can't always take time out, but mentally we can turn to God and ask for his help. By doing so, we will see the pressure for what it is, and will be in a far greater position to do something about it – not least with the help of others.

Thirdly, Jesus had the ability to use this potentially negative and harmful pressure for good, eg when a paralysed man was brought to him (Luke 5:17–26). Jesus told the man his sins were forgiven, which caused the Pharisees to question whether he had the right to do this. 'Who can forgive sins but God alone?' they asked. Yet Jesus used this situation to show he not only has power and authority to forgive sins but to heal. The man went away healed, the people were amazed and 'gave praise to God' and the Pharisees had no answer.

We too can use the pressure we face for the good. In the sports arena, when we are under pressure, we can ask Jesus to help us – it is surprising the difference that he can make to temperament and the ability to perform under pressure. When we see others under pressure, we can encourage and support them. When it comes to feeling pressure in life, perhaps because someone has questioned our faith in God, it can be an opportunity to share why our faith is important to us and the difference it can make to life.

Sport – Unihoc

Originating in Sweden, Unihoc takes elements of field and ice hockey to make a safe yet physically demanding game that can be played indoors by both men and women. It uses plastic sticks with flat heads and either a plastic puck or a light ball. The sticks, like those used in ice hockey, can be used on either side making it very easy for young people to play. It is now played in twenty countries worldwide and most secondary schools and sports centres have equipment that could be borrowed or hired.

Depending on the space you are playing in, you can chose if you want to play off the walls (like five-a-side football) or have the pitch boundaries of normal hockey. Unihoc is fast and furious and, for safety's sake, it may be worth reminding group members that they aren't playing golf and therefore don't have to swing their sticks wildly!

Value

Performing under pressure

Physical focus

Shooting

Game play priorities

Teamwork, communication, encouragement, discipline

Aim

To help group members recognise the value of being able to deal with pressure.

Learning objectives

To:

- recognise what causes pressure.
- To find out how to deal with pressure.
- To apply this to sport and life.

Equipment required

Unihoc sticks (enough for one each); unihoc balls/pucks (preferably one each – know how to adapt any practices if balls are in short supply); goals or cones to mark goals; bibs; cones to mark playing areas, use in warm up etc; a whistle.

Warm up

Dribble and shoot (5 mins)

All young people love to score goals, and this warm up gives them the opportunity! Have them dribble down the pitch and take a shot at goal. However, don't forget safety. Make sure they go down in turn two at a time, and, once they have both taken their shot, go and collect their ball (hopefully from the back of the net) and dribble back around the outside of the pitch while the next pair go.

Shooting tip – their feet need to be sideways on to the direction they want to shoot in.

Introduction and stretch

If appropriate, ask one of the young people (or a small group) to lead the stretching. It can be a good idea to ask them the week before. While stretching, find out what they remember from previous weeks.

Introduce this week's sports value – performing under pressure – and say that the physical focus will be shooting.

Skill

Three-way weave with shot (5 mins)
As Session 5, but this time with unihoc. Ask three people to line up and face down the pitch. The person in the middle (A) should start with the ball/puck. The person on the left (B) then runs into the middle, in front of A, and the ball /puck is passed to them (they should preferably run on to the pass). B then passes the ball/puck to the person on the right (C), who has run into the middle in front of them. In the meantime, A has run around the back of B on to the left wing, waiting to run into the middle and receive the pass from C. In the same way, B then runs around the back of C on to the right wing ready to receive the pass from A. This continues all the way up the pitch. When one of the three gets within range of the goal, they should have a shot.

Points you will need to emphasise about passing on the move:

• Pass ahead of the person so they can run on to the pass.

• Although you are on the move, you will need good control of the ball before you try to pass it.

• Your feet need to be sideways on to the way you wish to pass.

• Make sure you look up first.

Sports focus

Pressure and sport (10 mins)
Bring everyone together and sit down. Start with the question 'Has anyone experienced pressure in sport? If so, how has it affected you?' (Some may have felt under pressure taking their shots.) Add if not already given: **it can make us feel nervous**; **it can cause us to make mistakes**; **it can make us do things we regret later**.

Ask the question 'What should we do when we realise we are under pressure in sport?' Add if not already given: **recognise that everyone experiences it**; **take time out to recognise we are under pressure – sometimes this can be in the form of physical time out (eg basketball), while at other times it can only be a mental exercise**; **if playing in a team, share the pressure with someone else**; **use it to our advantage**; **ask God to help us cope**.

Game 1 is designed to put the group under pressure. As they reflect on how to deal with pressure, point out and encourage the game play priorities that you are looking for in the next game session – **teamwork**, **communication**, **encouragement**, **discipline** – and positively reinforce them when they occur.

Game 1

Team shooting (8 mins)
Divide the groups into teams and set each team up with a goal and a spot from behind which shots must be taken. Use cones to adjust the size of the goals depending on the ability of your group.

Each team member has to dribble up, take a shot from behind the marked spot, fetch their ball and get back to the team before the next person in their team can go. They will need to think about the play off between speed and accuracy. Award a point for every shot they get in, but take a point off for every one they miss. The first team to reach ten and sit down wins.

When repeating this game make changes such as, make the teams switch goals, dribble from the left/right instead of straight on etc. This will help to maintain the interest.

During this game, try to create pressure so they can experience what you have been talking about. Try handicapping teams so that they are under pressure to make up the difference, eg deduct a few points to start with so that a team is under pressure to make those points up; for another team, make it so they have to shoot at the goal from further away; you could even say that one team can only shoot left-handed (or right-handed if they are left-handed). Create pressure and see how each team copes. Remember to encourage the game play priorities.

At the end, make the point that pressure can be a real burden. How did they/could they have shared the pressure?

Life focus

Pressure and life! (10 mins)
Bring everyone together and sit down. Ask what some of the pressures we might face in life are. Add if not already given: **work deadlines**; **tests or exams**; **peer pressure**; **relationships – when people need our time or when someone we thought was a friend is unkind to us**.

How does pressure affect us? By making us: **lose our temper**; **scared**; **unable to sleep**; **unable to concentrate**.

How can we deal with that pressure? We need to: recognise that we will all experience pressure; identify it – what causes the pressure and how it affects us; share it with others; recognise God is with us and wants to help us deal with the pressure, so give the pressure to him through prayer.

Game 2

5 v 5 (12 mins)
Play a proper game of unihoc. Encourage them to put into practice the values and skills they have learned in the past sessions.

Cool down and wrap up

Don't forget to stretch!

Spotlight on the Bible

There are many areas of Christian life which can feel like a pressure: when people make fun of us for what we believe; wanting to be like everyone else; being tempted to do things that we know we shouldn't; feeling like we can't keep going.

When we feel under pressure, it is good to know that God promises that he is with us and will not let us 'go under'.

'When you pass through the waters,
I will be with you;
and when you pass through the rivers,
they will not sweep over you.
When you walk through the fire,
you will not be burned;
the flames will not set you ablaze.'
(Isaiah 43:2)

Reality check

'When are the times that I feel under pressure?'

'What could I do to try and help myself when I feel under pressure?'

'Do I provide care and support to my friends/family when they feel under pressure?'

Session 7

Working on our weaknesses

A We've all got weak areas. Perhaps you're great with your left foot but lousy with your right! Or you find it easy to throw a ball, but catching is a different matter. Maybe you have a real temper, and it doesn't take much to get you really riled. Or perhaps you are so ambitious that anyone who stands in your way is brushed aside as if they don't matter.

People often deal with their weak areas in one of three ways: some people ignore them and never attempt to do anything about them; some recognise them, but aren't prepared to work at them; or they see them, work at them over a period of time and change. God wants us to be whole, balanced people. That is not to say we are not going to have weaknesses, but with his help, we can work at those weak areas.

'... My grace is sufficient for you, my power is made perfect in weakness.'
(2 Corinthians 12:9)

The Bible recognises that there will be areas in our lives where we are weak, which Jesus wants to help us to work on. When Jesus met Zacchaeus, the tax collector, he wanted to help him, amongst other things, overcome his habit of stealing (Luke 19:1–10). Whether it is a bad temper that comes out whilst playing a sport, or stealing from others, Jesus can help us overcome our weaknesses.

There will be other weaknesses in our lives, things like being nervous when speaking in public or a particular illness, where Jesus calls us to lean on him. He offers us not only the help we need to cope but promises us that his power will be seen all the more as a result of our weakness.

In this session, the important thing is to help the group members recognise the areas in sport and life where they are weak and to help them to develop as individuals.

If, for example, someone can't pass with their left foot, spend time helping them do this so that they begin the process of feeling confident about doing so, rather than never attempting it. In life, it may be that they have a bad temper, or that they don't always tell the truth. Help them to recognise the areas where they might be weak, but also help them to see how they can change. Here are three practical ways.

Firstly, they need to acknowledge their weakness before God and ask him to help them change.

Secondly, they need discipline to work on their areas of weakness – eg when they find themselves about to do things they recognise as being wrong, stopping themselves.

Thirdly, having someone to be accountable to – telling someone they love and respect of the areas they want to work on, so that this person can challenge and help when needed.

Sport – Football

Football, the beautiful game! Former Liverpool manager Bill Shankley is famously quoted as saying, 'Some people think football is a matter of life and death ... I can assure them it is much more serious than that.'

Football is by far the most widely played and watched team sport in this country, and there are very few people who are immune to the football culture in the UK – just look at the response during the World Cup. However, the football players who reach iconic status are not necessarily always the role models we might choose for our young people. Trouble off the pitch is widely reported, and often their on-the-pitch behaviour is far from what we might aim for as we think about 'Christian sporting attitudes'. The problem is that, due to the high profile of football, what young people see footballers doing will play a key role in what they think sportsmanship is all about. This means that it is especially difficult for young people to come up with a sporting attitude that is different to the one they see displayed by the professionals, and it is VITAL that we seek to apply the values we address to football.

B Value

Working on our weaknesses

Physical focus

Evaluating and improving our performance

Game play priorities

Persistence, working at things we find difficult

Aim

To help group members recognise the value of working on our weak areas.

Learning objectives

To:

- learn how to assess yourself honestly.
- To work at the weak areas identified.
- To learn to tackle one area at a time.

Equipment required

Footballs (preferably one each, know how to adapt any practices if balls are in short supply); any other equipment you think they might need; goals or cones to mark goals; bibs; cones to mark playing areas and use in warm up; a whistle.

Warm up and skill

Three-way weave with shot (6 mins)
This is the same as the skill done in Session 6 but played with footballs instead of unihoc.

Introduction and stretch

Get one of the young people (or a small group) to lead the stretching. Find out what they remember from previous sessions.

Introduce this week's sports value – working at our weaknesses – and say that today you'll be looking at evaluating and improving our performance.

Game 1

Devise a practise exercise (8 mins)
Group members should decide what they need to work on – passing, dribbling, spacing, attacking, defending, shooting – and get into groups to do this. The task is then to devise a fun practice exercise that will work to improve

that area. It is OK for them to base their ideas on a practice exercise they already know, but they should be able to identify how it helps them improve the skill they have decided to work on. Say that later they will be expected to teach another group their exercise, and together they will evaluate its effectiveness.

Sports focus

Learning new skills in sport (8 mins)
Bring everyone together and sit down. Begin by asking the question 'Which foot do you prefer to kick with?' or 'Which hand do you throw with?' Point out that it's easy to become secure with what we are good at in sport, and not to work on the areas where perhaps we are weak.

Ask what you need to do to excel at a sport. Add if not already given: **work on all aspects of the game**; **work particularly hard at your weaker areas**; **be willing to receive helpful criticism**.

How can we work on our weak areas? Add if not already given: **identify what they are**; **ask for help from your coach or team mates**; **work on them – don't give up**.

Ask them if they enjoy working at the things they find hard. Stress the importance of being able to receive constructive feedback – this is what will happen next! The game play priorities for this session include persistence and working hard at areas they find difficult.

Game 2

Evaluate and improve (10 mins)
Join groups together to quickly teach each other their practice exercises.

Each group should:

• identify the area they are trying to improve with their exercise

• teach the exercise to the other group and let them try it quickly

• join with the other group to evaluate the exercise's effectiveness in terms of how successful and enjoyable it is

• work with the other group to come up with ways in which it could be improved.

Make sure they get a chance to evaluate both groups' exercises. You may need to encourage them to swap over, so that they don't run out of time.

Life focus

Learning new skills in life (8 mins)
Bring everyone together and sit down. Begin by asking, 'What are some possible weak areas in life?' Add if not already given examples like: **a bad temper**; **indiscipline**; **negative behaviour**.

What can we do about our weak areas? Add if not already given: **identify what they are**; **ask your family and friends to help**; **be prepared to work at weak areas**; **be disciplined**; **ask God to help us change**.

Game 3

Five-a-side football (10 mins)
Play a short game of football. As they play ask them to think about whether they chose the right areas to work on, and whether the extra practice resulted in any improvement. It will usually take more than one training session to really see improvement!

Praise them for being prepared to work on the areas where they are weak – it takes courage. Remind them that they have only been practising for a short length of time – encourage them to think how much more they will grow in the areas where they are weak as they continue to practise.

Cool down and wrap up

Don't forget to stretch!

Spotlight on the Bible

Having weaknesses is not a problem if we are willing to hand them over to God and let him work on them. Often we find it easier to surrender the things we struggle with, because we know we cannot cope by ourselves and have to ask God to help us.

'But he said to me, "My grace is sufficient for you, for my power is made perfect in weakness." Therefore I will boast all the more gladly about my weaknesses, so that Christ's power may rest on me.'
(2 Corinthians 12:9)

Reality check

'Do I automatically give up when I find something hard?'

'Can I listen to constructive feedback and use it to help me improve?'

'What areas do I want to improve in my life – at home, at school, with friends?'

'What am I going to do to try to improve those areas?'

Session 8

Enjoyment

A Sport and life are gifts. It's easy to take for granted the ability to go out and run around and to have the energy to live life to the full. Yet, so often, many of these pleasures are lost amidst the pressure of life, whether in the sports arena, in the classroom or at work. In Session 6, on performing under pressure, we were reminded of what some of those pressures are for young people today. This session seeks to remind us that ultimately sport and life are given to enjoy, not to burden us.

The Bible tells us that God's desire is that we experience life to the full. Jesus said, 'I have come that they may have life and have it to the full' (John 10:10). By saying this, he didn't mean that we would all suddenly find our diaries overloaded, or that life should be one big party, with lots of froth but little depth. Ultimately, he was talking about the joy and the privilege that comes from having a relationship with God, through Jesus. Only then will we find purpose for living, a true perspective on life, a sense of joy, freedom and security.

Jesus showed us how to live life to the full:

- In his ability to enjoy life, eg the wedding party (John 2:1–11), socialising in people's homes (Luke 19:1–9).
- In his ability to focus on what was good and true.
- In his constant desire to be in touch with the creator of life – God.

The main aim of this session is to help the group members recognise the fact that sport is a gift to be enjoyed. If we lose, we aren't going to die or be shunned by our friends. It is given for us to enjoy, and we are fortunate to be able to play sport. The word 'sport' means to 'enjoy' and 'to have fun'.

Of course, there are times in life that are hard – failed exams, a death in the family etc. However, that doesn't take away the fact that life is a gift, one that God wants to share with us. Help group members to see those things in life that are good, eg friends and family, their abilities, the wonders of creation etc.

Sport – Non-stop cricket

Non-stop cricket is an easier and faster moving variation of the game of cricket, and many of the young people will have played it at school.

Underarm bowling means it is easier to hit the ball, and being allowed to bowl the ball, even if the batter isn't back at the stumps, makes it fast moving. If the group particularly enjoy using their football skills, the game can be adapted by rolling a football at the wicket and the 'batter' kicking the ball instead.

B Value

Enjoyment

Physical focus

Fielding skills

Game play priorities

Not taking the game too seriously, encouragement, fair play

Aim

To help group members recognise the true value of enjoying sport and life.

Learning objectives

To:

- recognise the enjoyment that sport and life bring
- recognise the privilege of playing sport and enjoying life
- apply these values to all aspects of life.

Equipment required

Cricket bats (preferably two for every game you will have running); wickets (one for each game you will be running – use a board propped up against a bin if necessary); balls (preferably one each – alter Skills and Game 1 according to the number of balls you have – proper indoor cricket windballs are the best but tennis balls can be used); cones/markers (at least three for every game you will have running); a whistle.

Warm up and skill

Give the group the opportunity to get used to handling a cricket ball (if you are using them). Practise throwing in the air and catching, with the little fingers or thumbs together. See how many times they can clap before catching the ball. If you have plenty of space, work in pairs, seeing how far apart they can get while still throwing and catching the ball accurately.

Introduction and stretch

Get one of the young people (or a small group) to lead the stretching. Find out what they remember from previous sessions.

Introduce this week's sports value – enjoyment – and say that today you'll be playing non-stop cricket and working on your fielding skills.

Game 1

Fielding skills races (8 mins)

- In pairs, with one opposite the other, roll the ball backwards and forwards to each other ten times using a 'long barrier' to stop the ball. To do this, kneel one leg down at right angles to the direction the ball is travelling in – use your leg, body and arms to make a barrier that will stop the ball even if it bounces as it comes towards you. The first pair to finish wins.

• As above, but throw the ball to each other. If you are trying to catch the ball below chest-height, your little fingers should be together; above chest-height and your thumbs should be together. Don't have wrists together and fingers pointing towards the ball, as if you mistime it, it is very easy to hurt fingers this way! First pair to make ten throws (without dropping any) wins.

• As above, but vary the distance between the players. The further apart the players are, the more difficult it is to make an accurate throw.

• Standing one behind the other, the first person rolls the ball away from the pair. The second person has to run after it, pick it up, and throw it back to their partner and return to the starting position. Then swap roles. The skill is in being able to scoop up the ball, turn and throw it accurately back in one smooth action. The first team to do this ten times (without dropping any) wins.

There are numerous drills that you can do that practise general throwing, catching and fielding – feel free to be creative!

Sports focus

Fun and sport (8 mins)
Bring everyone together and sit down. Begin by asking the question: 'What do you enjoy about sport?' Receive answers with affirmation and add if not already given: **the word sport means fun** (it's a shortening of 'disport' which means 'to enjoy oneself'); **fun to play with other people**; **fun to learn a skill**; **fun to face a challenge**; **fun to compete**.

Explain that it's easy to lose sight of sport being fun. Ask what will help us remember. Add if not already given: **not taking sport so seriously**; **learning to win and lose well**; **appreciating others less fortunate than ourselves**; **recognising that working at our weak areas will help to make sport more fun**; **appreciating the gifts that God has given us**.

Game 2

Non-stop cricket (12 mins)
Set the pitch up with a cone for the bowler to bowl from, a wicket and a cone out to either side of the wicket.

The batter scores a 'run' every time they go around one of the cones. They have to run around a cone every time they hit the ball (even if it isn't a very good hit). If it is a good hit or the ball is misfielded, they can keep running around both cones and score more points. Like ordinary cricket, the batter is 'out' if they are caught or if the bowler manages to hit the wicket.

The reason this is called non-stop cricket is that the bowler can bowl as soon as they get the ball back – they don't have to wait for the batter to be ready. When the batter is out, the next team member needs to run in quickly, as the bowler can bowl as soon as they have the ball at the bowling mark. The batting team therefore need to line up in a safe place, out of the way of the wicketkeeper, but close enough to be able to run in to take over when necessary.

Depending on the ability of your group, you can add additional rules such as you have to bowl underarm, you can't be out on your first ball etc.

If you are going to have timed innings, you may have to have a set number of runs at which a player has to declare and hand on to the next player in order to make sure that everybody gets

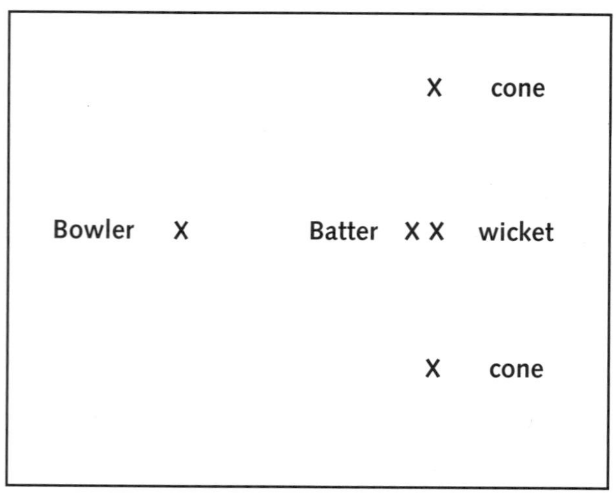

the opportunity to bat. If you get through all the players before the time is up, you can either say that any who have declared get another go or that you simply start again at the beginning of the batting order and continue through until the time is up. By counting the number of people who are out, this can act as a tie-breaker in the event of both teams finishing with the same score.

Life focus

Fun and life (8 mins)
Bring everyone together and sit down. Begin by asking, 'What are some of the things that are good about life?' Receive answers with affirmation, adding if not already given: **friends**; **family**; **chocolate**; **good health**; **sunshine**.

Ask, 'How can we enjoy life?' Add if not already mentioned: **by appreciating the things we sometimes take for granted – air to breathe, bodies, friends and family**; **by playing fairly in life** (remind them of Session 3 on fair play); **by keeping the right perspective on what is important and what isn't**; **by being positive and looking at what is good**; **including others**; **listening to God and obeying his teaching**.

Explain how God intended life to be fun. In John 10:10, Jesus says 'I have come that they may have life, and have it to the full.' He can open our eyes to what is good in all he has created, and he gives us rules for living to make it fun – he shows us what will really satisfy.

As you reflect on 'enjoyment', point out and encourage this session's game play priorities. This session they are: **not to take the game too seriously**, **to play fairly** and **to encourage one another**.

Game 3

Non-stop cricket (10 mins)
Have a second innings of non-stop cricket. If the teams were very uneven, use this opportunity to alter them as appropriate.

Cool down and wrap up

Don't forget to stretch!

Spotlight on the Bible

God promises to help us have joy in life by his Holy Spirit.

> *'... the fruit of the Spirit is love, joy, peace, patience, kindness, goodness, faithfulness, gentleness and self-control. Against such things there is no law.' (Galatians 5:22,23)*

Indeed Paul prays for the church in Rome:

> *'May the God of hope fill you with all joy and peace as you trust in him, so that you may overflow with hope by the power of the Holy Spirit.' (Romans 15:13)*

Reality check

'Do I manage to have fun while I play sport?'

'Does the way I play and the attitude I have help others to have fun?'

'Are there other areas in my life that I need to learn to take less seriously and learn to enjoy?'

Session 9

Persistence

A Have you ever wondered what it is that keeps a long distance runner going and going? There is only one word for it – persistence. The Bible places great value on persistence. Paul says:

> *'I press on towards the goal to win the prize for which God has called me heavenwards in Christ Jesus.' (Philippians 3:14)*

In sport, as with life, there are many times when the easy option seems to be to give up. Certainly, many professional sportsmen and women will have had times when that has seemed the most attractive option. But in order to perform to the highest level in the sports world, persistence is essential.

It is vital in other aspects of life, too – working at a particular subject, applying for a particular job or working at a relationship. Persistence is something that will often take us through those times when we feel like giving up. It is a value worth having!

There were many obstacles put in Jesus' way throughout his life that could have made him give up, but he kept on going. What was it that caused Jesus to be so persistent?

Jesus had a clear aim. He knew he had been called by God to fulfil his work. He found strength to keep going from God, even at the point of death (Matthew 26:42).

More importantly, Jesus was clear of his calling (Matthew 4:23). He knew what God had called him to do. When we believe in what we are doing, we are given a greater incentive to stick at it even when times are hard.

Another factor for Jesus' persistence was the knowledge that God was with him (John 10:38). When we know others are with us, especially Jesus, we are given greater encouragement to push through the challenging times. Jesus assures us we will never be alone (Matthew 28:20). He gives us his Holy Spirit (Acts 2) to assure us of this each day and to help us.

This session explores the value of persistence in sport and life, and helps group members to understand how they can apply this value to their lives. In relation to sport, persistence comes from the inner desire to do your best and try your hardest. It will come from not wanting to let yourself or others down. It will come when you believe in something. Persistence is something we constantly have to work at.

When it comes to life, explain that there will be many occasions when it will be all too easy to give up. Help group members to see that, by being prepared to work at such things, we will grow as people.

Sport – Basketball

Basketball is experiencing major growth in this country with increasing free access to outdoor courts, and has a definite 'cool factor' attached to it. Dr James Naismith invented basketball in 1891. The aim was to devise a new indoor game that would provide an 'athletic distraction' for a rowdy class at the YMCA in Springfield, Massachusetts, USA, and take their minds off the New England winter.

It was originally played with nine players on each side, and the aim was to score by shooting into old peach baskets that were nailed to the lower rail of the gym balcony – hence 'basket' ball. It became an Olympic sport in 1936 and is now played by more than 300 million people worldwide.

Value

Persistence

Physical focus

Shooting

Game play priorities

Not giving up, encouraging one another

Aim

To teach the value of never giving up.

Learning objectives:

To recognise:

- the need for persistence.
- how to be persistent, and how to apply it to your life.

Equipment required

Baskets (think in advance about how you will split the group around baskets for games); basketballs (preferably one each, have appropriate sizes); bibs; cones/hoops to make extra game areas if necessary (see Session 3); a whistle.

Warm up

Let the young people play and practise their shooting while you wait for everybody to arrive. This also gives you an opportunity to assess their ability.

Introduction and stretch

Get one of the young people (or a small group) to lead the stretching. Find out what they remember from previous sessions.

Introduce this week's sports value – persistence – and say that today you'll be playing basketball and working on your shooting skills.

Skill

Set shot (8 mins)
Think **BEEF**.

- **Balance** – Feet shoulder width apart, facing the basket, knees bent.
- **Eyes** – Look at the basket, eyes under the ball (if strong enough to shoot this way) – this encourages you to hold the ball above your head which makes it less easy to be checked when shooting. (Many young people naturally bring the ball down to chest height before they shoot. If they are strong enough to shoot without doing this it should be encouraged.)

• **Elbow** – 90° perpendicular to the floor, in front of body not sticking out to the side (initially can feel strange – persevere!). NB the other hand is only on the side of the ball to support it and provide strength in case the shot is checked; it is not involved in shooting.

• **Follow through** or **flick** – the shot should start in the legs, and then be pushed all the way up, ending with a push through the wrist, flicking the fingers forward to get backspin on the ball. This not only helps the flight of the ball, but also means the shot is more likely to spin in if it hits the ring.

As they practise shooting, go around helping, encouraging and correcting individuals as necessary.

Game 1

Shooting game (5 mins)
Get into teams of four to five. Say that you're going to have a relay race, and that there will be two points for a basket (you may want to give them one point if they hit the ring or the small black square if their shooting still needs a lot of work).

Give each team a ball, mark a spot for them to shoot from, and tell them to collect their own rebounds and give the ball to the next person in the queue. The first team to score ten points and sit down quietly wins.

Play through a couple of times. You could handicap the scores as appropriate, eg the winning team has to get twelve in the next game, the losing team eight, while others stay at ten.

Don't forget the game play priorities. This session they are not giving up, even if another team goes into the lead you need to keep going and be persistent, and encouragement, building one another up in the team verbally, encouraging them to keep trying even if they find it hard.

Positively reinforce these when you see them during the game.

Sports focus

Persistence and sport (8 mins)
Bring everyone together and sit down. Begin by asking for examples in sport where there is the need for persistence. Add or bring out these points: **we need persistence in sport when we are training; when we feel we have failed; and when it seems likely we are going to lose a game, and are tempted to give up**.

Ask how we can help ourselves not to give up. **Be determined/disciplined; be positive; remember the game is not over until the final whistle**.

How can we help others not to give up? **By encouragement, both practical and vocal; by sharing our own experiences; by physical and emotional support**.

Encourage them to put into practice what they have just been working on. Their shooting may not improve immediately; they need persistence!

Game 2

45° rebound shot (5 mins)
Demonstrate the rebound shot – the easiest shot. Stand at a 45° angle to the basket, stand one BIG stride back from the basket, and aim to hit the top corner of the little black square – it should go in every time!

Play the relay game in teams, with the same rules as before, but shooting from the rebound position.

Life focus

Persistence and life (8 mins)
Bring everyone together and sit down. Begin by asking what areas in life you sometimes feel like giving up in. Add or bring out these examples: **exams**; **sport – perhaps a particular**

sport is hard to learn; **family**; **school – school work, or perhaps bullying**; **friends**.

Ask how we can keep going: **tell others we are struggling and ask for help**; **look to positively change the situation**; **believe things will get better**.

Point out how God can help: **he is with us**; **he gives us the strength we need, not only to cope, but to conquer**; **he gives us people to support us**.

Also point out the game play priorities that you will be looking for in the next game – **not giving up** and **encouraging one another**.

Game 3

Half court 3 v 3 (14 mins)
As Session 3.

Cool down and wrap up

Don't forget to stretch!

Spotlight on the Bible

There is a story in the Bible about a widow who, by her persistence, gets justice from the local judge (Luke 18:1–5). Jesus used the story to encourage people to have persistence when they pray:

> *'And will not God bring about justice for his chosen ones, who cry out to him day and night? Will he keep putting them off? I tell you, he will see that they get justice, and quickly.' (Luke 18:7,8)*

Is there something that you feel strongly enough about, that you want to pray until you see things change? It will take persistence.

Reality check

'Do I help others to keep going even when they are struggling?'

'Is there one specific thing that I want to try harder at this week?'

'Do I give up too easily in sport, at school, when I'm faced with something hard?'

Session 10

Being a leader

A Leadership can be seen as something that's only for the chosen few. When it comes to actively being chosen to lead a team in sport, or to be head of school, or a manager at work, the qualities needed to lead are ones we should all strive for.

Think about leaders who have inspired you – a parent, a football player or perhaps a politician. What was it about that person that caused you to take note of the way they led? Jesus has inspired millions of people over the years. He was a natural leader of men and women. Jesus says of the leader, 'the greatest among you should be like the youngest, and one who rules like the one who serves' (Luke 22:26). There are three qualities recognisable in Jesus that we need to apply to our own lives in order to take seriously what it means to be a leader.

Firstly, Jesus was a positive role model. When we look at his life, we can respect him in the way he lived his life, the things he said, and in what he asks of us.

Secondly, Jesus was an encourager and inspirer. There is great value in encouragement. Encourage someone to do something and more often than not they will do it, and grow in doing so.

Thirdly, Jesus was a server. That might seem a strange quality, but in reality we will only be able to ask of others what we are prepared to do ourselves.

The important aspect of this session is that the young people recognise that we are called to be leaders whether we are chosen to lead a group of people or not. Help the group to see that when it comes to the sports arena, it means being prepared to look at the way we conduct ourselves amongst our friends and the other team. It means being prepared to be part of the team, building others up, not knocking them down, and helping others develop their game rather than simply being concerned about ourselves.

When it comes to life, help the group to see that many of the values you have addressed in relation to sport apply to the home, to the classroom, to work and to relationships etc.

Sport – Tournament

Choose whatever sport the group enjoys playing the most.

Value

Being a leader

Game play priorities

Being a positive role model, fair play, working at skill, encouragement

Aim

To teach the values necessary for leadership in sport and life.

Learning objectives

To:

- recognise the responsibility of leadership.
- enable group members to feel more able to lead.
- lead by example.

Equipment required

The equipment required for your group's favourite sport; ideas about order of play; score sheet to keep track of results; bibs; cones/hoops to make extra game areas if necessary; a whistle.

Warm up and skill

Use a practice exercise that the group is familiar with, that is related to the sport you have chosen. NB By this stage the group should be able to choose a practice that will warm them up and prepare them for the tournament – let them choose their own if appropriate.

Introduction and stretch

Ask one of the young people (or a small group) to lead the stretching.

Introduce this week's sports value – being a leader – and say that as today is the final session, the physical focus will be a tournament. Say you want to see them putting everything they have thought about so far in the course into practice. What kind of things will they be?

Game 1

Tournament (8 mins)

Decide whether it is best to do a version of the game for small teams or have a full game, depending on numbers and space available etc.

Put them into teams of roughly equal ability. Ask each team to choose who they want their captain to be. Play a mini tournament of your chosen sport – a round robin format where every team plays every other team will work best, unless you have a large number of teams. When thinking of the time allowed for each game, remember not to have people sitting off for too long. This may also affect your decision for small teams or a full game.

There is no need to complete all the games in this section, as Game 2 and Game 3 will provide more time for tournament play.

Be ready to positively reinforce the game play priorities for this session – **being a positive role model, playing fairly, encouraging those in the team** and **working at skill**.

Sports focus

Leadership and sport (8 mins)
Bring everyone together and sit down. Begin by asking the question 'Who are the leaders in sport that stand out to you?' Go on to ask what some of the qualities of a leader are. Receive answers with affirmation and add or bring out these points: **being good at playing the game – someone who is respected because of the way they play physically; good at encouraging players – a good leader of people; a good role model – someone who is respected because of the way they play rather than their ability.**

Pick out three qualities of a leader in sport, eg **they need to lead by example and be role models; they need to have the respect of the team; they need to be able to bring out the best in people.**

Game 2

Tournament (cont) (8 mins)
Carry on with the tournament, but ask each team to choose another captain, to give as many people the chance to experience being the leader as possible.

During this time, help group members to recognise and put into practice qualities required in leaders.

These are areas to work at: being a positive role model; playing fairly; encouraging those in the team; working at skill.

Life focus

Leadership and life! (8 mins)
Bring everyone together and sit down. Start by asking how the qualities of being a leader in sport relate to being a leader in life. Add or bring out these points: **we're all called to display the qualities of a leader in the way we live out our lives; we're all called to encourage and serve one another; we're called to be positive role models.**

Ask how they can put this into practice? **By helping in the home; by treating others as they themselves would like to be treated; by checking what they say and do.**

Point out the qualities that Jesus had as a leader: **positive role model; team player; fair and loyal; clear direction; a servant.**

Game 3

Tournament (cont) (8 mins)
Again, ask the teams to choose another captain. Finish the tournament. If you have extra time, do some team shooting games/races.

Cool down and wrap up

Don't forget to stretch!

Spotlight on the Bible

What does it mean to have Jesus as our leader? Jesus says:

> *'If anyone would come after me, he must deny himself and take up his cross daily and follow me.' (Luke 9:23)*

This means that following Jesus involves doing what you think he would want you to do, even when it is difficult. However, the reward for following Jesus is knowing that we will be with him forever, and that nothing can snatch us from his hand (John 10:27,28).

Reality check

'How can I be a positive role model at home, at school, with my friends?'

'How do I want to be different and what am I going to do to try to make a change?'

'What aspect of the course do I think I most need to work on personally?' (It may be a good idea to quickly remind them of the different sessions.)

Close

As this is the final session, use the opportunity to explain that you have chosen to have Jesus as the leader of your life, and what differences it has made to you.

This session should effectively wrap up the whole course. Consider the areas you think are key for your group, and focus on those. If there was one thing you wanted your group to take from the course, what would it be? If appropriate, you could challenge the group about choosing Jesus to be the leader of their lives.

Following this, some of the young people may want to say a prayer of commitment:

'Father God, thank you for loving me. Thank you for demonstrating that love through the death of your son, Jesus, on the cross. Please forgive me for all the wrong things I do that separate me from your love. Thank you that because of Jesus' death I can know your forgiveness and that because Jesus rose again I can know you as my father. Help me to live a new life, with you at the centre. Please fill me with your Spirit, to be my guide and helper, especially when I'm struggling to do what is right. Please be a part of my life from now on. In Jesus' name, Amen.'

Finally, if you are going to continue running sessions with the *Fit for Life Course* (see p 48) let them know when and where it is!

The Fit for Life Course

Take ten topical themes. Mix in some wisdom from the Bible. Add some fun sporting activities. And you have the *Fit for Life Course*!

With its use of non-jargon terms and friendly sporting activities, the *Fit for Life Course* is the ideal companion to the *Sports Value Course*. It builds on the format used, but this time starting from life issues as opposed to values found in sport.

In ten, tried and tested, sport-based sessions, topical themes such as homelessness, money and self-worth are looked at. Each session contains a biblical introduction, sporting activities and discussions, all of which exercise both the body and the mind.

Ideal for youth groups everywhere!

ISBN: 1 85999 6493

£6.99

Available January 2004 from all good Christian bookshops or from

Scripture Union (Mail Order), PO Box 5148, Milton Keynes MLO, MK2 2YX
Tel (01908) 856006 or from

www.scriptureunion.org.uk